Need to Know

Asthma

Jenny Bryan

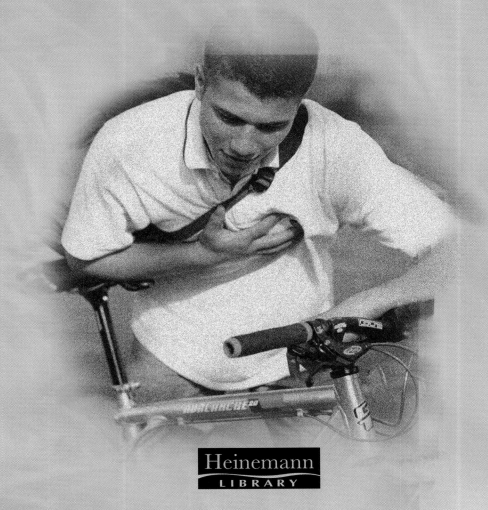

Heinemann
LIBRARY

H **www.heinemann.co.uk/library**
Visit our website to find out more information about **Heinemann Library** books.

To order:
 Phone 44 (0) 1865 888066
 Send a fax to 44 (0) 1865 314091
 Visit the Heinemann Bookshop at www.heinemann.co.uk/library to browse our
catalogue and order online.

Produced by Monkey Puzzle Media Ltd
Gissing's Farm, Fressingfield, Suffolk IP21 5SH, UK

First published in Great Britain by Heinemann
Library, Halley Court, Jordan Hill, Oxford OX2 8EJ,
part of Harcourt Education.
Heinemann is a registered trademark of Harcourt
Education Ltd.

Editorial: Katie Orchard
Design: Jane Hawkins
Picture Research: Sally Cole
Consultant: The National Asthma Campaign
Production: Viv Hichens

Originated by Ambassador Litho Ltd
Printed and bound in Hong Kong, China by
 South China Printing Company

ISBN 0 431 09761 5
08 07 06 05 04
10 9 8 7 6 5 4 3 2 1

British Library Cataloguing in Publication Data
Bryan, Jenny
 Asthma. - (Need to know)
 1.Asthma - Juvenile literature
 I.Title
 616.2'38

Acknowledgements
The publishers would like to thank the following for
permission to reproduce photographs:
AKG pp. 6, 8 (San Meyer); Alamy p. 47 (Dave
Seigel); Corbis pp. 11 (Sygma), 15 (Patrick Ward),
20 (Norbert Schaefer), 22 (Ariel Skelley), 33
(Michael Keller), 36–37 (Richard T. Nowitz); Digital
Vision p. 26; Getty Images pp. 39 (Stone), 43 (Taxi);
Mary Evans Picture Library p. 9; Photofusion p. 16
(Brian Mitchell); Rex Features pp. 34 (Reso), 42
(Tim Rooke); Science Photo Library pp. 1 (Mark
Clarke), 4 (Matthew Munro), 10 (Antonia Reeve),
12 (Innerspace Imaging), 13 (Mark Clarke), 18
(BSIP Ducloux), 21 (Andrew Syred), 23 (Leonard
Lessin/FBPA), 24 (A. Glauberman), 28 (Damien
Lovegrove), 29 (Damien Lovegrove), 30 (Bill Aron),
35 (CC Studio), 45 (James King-Holmes/ICRF), 46
(CNRI), 48 (NIBSC), 50 (P. Plailly/Eurelios); Topham
Picturepoint pp. 5 (Bob Daemmrich/ImageWorks),
25 (ImageWorks), 27, 40 (AP), 49 (ImageWorks).

Cover photographs reproduced courtesy of Robert
Harding Picture Library and Science Photo
Library/Andrew Syred.

Contents

Any words appearing in the text in bold, **like this**, are explained in the Glossary.

Introducing asthma

Asthma does not stop people from enjoying sport, as long as it is kept under control.

Around the world, about 150 million people have asthma – about one in ten children and one in 20 adults. It has become steadily more common over the last 20 years, especially in developed countries, such as the UK, USA and Australia.

Asthma is a breathing problem. It affects the lungs – two vital organs that lie in the chest, one on either side of the heart, protected by the ribcage. Inside each lung is a network of small tubes (the airways), which carry air in and out of the body. People who have asthma cannot always breathe easily. This happens when some of their airways become narrower and close up so that air cannot get in and out properly. This makes people wheeze and short of breath. Their chest feels tight, as if there is a big elastic band around it.

Asthma usually starts in childhood. Some children grow out of it, but others do not. Some only have difficulty breathing when they are near something that irritates their airways. Others always have breathing problems, wherever they are, if their asthma is uncontrolled.

Controlling asthma

There are some very effective medicines for asthma. Most are breathed into the lungs through devices called inhalers. Some medicines, called relievers, make it easier for people to breathe when they have asthma symptoms. Others, called preventers, are taken to prevent asthma. Although there are good treatments available, asthma can be very serious and even fatal. It is important for people with asthma to use their inhalers, even when they feel well. Breathing problems sometimes happen suddenly and there may not be time to get to hospital.

Most people with asthma lead full, active lives. They play sport, go to parties and hang out with their friends without their asthma getting in the way. They make sure that they are in charge of their health, so their asthma fits in with what they want to do, and not the other way around.

"When I was a little kid, I don't remember not having asthma. Asthma was a stress-induced thing for me. And it was an every day thing. It was something I lived with, but it wasn't a big deal. I still played sports, but I would just have attacks and have to be hospitalized every now and then. I knew it wasn't normal, but it was normal for me."

(Grammy award winning rap artist, Coolio)

History of asthma

Treatments for asthma have not always been as effective as they are today. In ancient Egypt, around 1550 BCE, people with asthma might have had their intestines washed out with a cleansing solution called an **enema**. Worse still, breathing problems were sometimes treated with camel or crocodile dung smeared on their chests! Just a few centuries later, in 1000 BCE, the Chinese discovered a much more effective treatment – a plant called *Ma Huang*. This plant contained a drug called **ephedrine**, which was used to treat asthma well into the 20th century.

Early studies of asthma

The best description of asthma in ancient times came from the Greek physician, Aretaeus of Cappadocia (81–131 CE), who described its symptoms as: 'heaviness of the chest, sluggishness to one's accustomed work and to every other exertion, difficulty in breathing on a steep road … they breathe standing as if desiring to draw all the air which they can possibly inhale and they also open the mouth …'

In South America, the root of the ipecacuanha plant was used as a medicine to relieve coughing.

A thousand years later, the Jewish physician, Moses Maimonides (1130–1204), wrote the first book about asthma. He recommended that people with asthma should live in climates where the air is dry and that they remain calm, avoiding anything exciting, including sex. He advised against sleeping during an asthma attack and proposed chicken soup as a remedy.

Asthma treatments throughout history

In the search for a cure for asthma, many weird and wonderful remedies have been suggested throughout history, including:

- animal dung
- herbs, such as squill and henbane
- making people vomit
- extracting blood out of veins
- enemas
- powdered fox's lung (taken dissolved as liquid medicine)
- breathing dry air
- avoiding feathers
- sleeping upright on a chair.

New discoveries

Mixed progress in the treatment of asthma continued through the **Middle Ages** and the European **Renaissance**. Exploratory travel across the Atlantic to the Americas led to the discovery of a Brazilian shrub, ipecacuanha, whose dried root relieved coughing. The same voyages of exploration also brought tobacco, which was initially recommended for the treatment of lung ailments. Today we know that tobacco triggers breathing problems.

Breakthroughs in the 17th century

Many of the 17th-century doctors who studied asthma had the condition themselves. One of these – an English physician called Sir John Floyer – described two types of asthma, 'continued' (constant) and 'periodic' (occasional). He started to understand that narrowing of the airways in the lungs was important and realized that, for people with asthma, breathing out was as much a problem as breathing in. He also noticed that family history, weather, seasons, pollution, tobacco smoke, infection, exercise and emotions could all affect asthma.

Making progress

As 18th- and 19th-century researchers learned more about the structure of the lungs, asthma treatments became more logical. In 1808, the European researcher, Franz Reisseisen, showed that there was a layer of muscle around the airways in the lungs. He also noted that when the muscle **contracted** (became smaller and tighter), the airways became narrower.

In 1816, the French physician, Rene Laennec, invented the **stethoscope**. This allowed doctors to listen to what was happening inside the chest. By listening to the chests of people with asthma, Laennec became convinced that they were getting **spasms** (involuntary contractions) in the muscles of their airways. This made their airways twitch, stiffen and close up. In 1846 came the discovery of another important piece of medical equipment – the **spirometer**. This allowed doctors to measure the strength of a person's lungs and how much air they could breathe out. Spirometers are still widely used today. People breathe out into a mouthpiece as hard as they can, so that doctors can measure how well their lungs are working.

In 1860, an asthmatic English doctor, Henry Hyde Salter, wrote about his research on several hundred patients and realized that asthma tended to be worse when people were asleep. He recommended strong, black coffee to treat asthma attacks.

Stethoscope design has changed little since Rene Laennec's first model. This one was made in 1819.

Salter also showed that asthma responded to belladonna (deadly nightshade), which we know today is very poisonous. In fact, it was a chemical called atropine, contained in belladonna, which was helping to relieve asthma attacks.

In 1892, the English physician, Sir William Osler, described three mechanisms of asthma, which form the basis for many of today's treatments for the disease. He proposed that asthma was caused by muscle spasm, **inflammation** and abnormal nerve activity in the airways. In the early part of the 20th century, other scientists produced a variety of drugs to relieve muscle spasm and improve nerve activity in the airways. These drugs included **adrenaline** and ephedrine, and a caffeine-type drug called aminophylline. But it would be another 50 years before researchers discovered how to tackle inflammation.

It also took time to find the best way to deliver asthma medication directly to the airways. In the 1950s the asthmatic daughter of the president of a US **pharmaceutical company** asked her father why her medicine could not be put in a spray-can like hair lacquer. It was not long before scientists developed the prototype for today's inhalers.

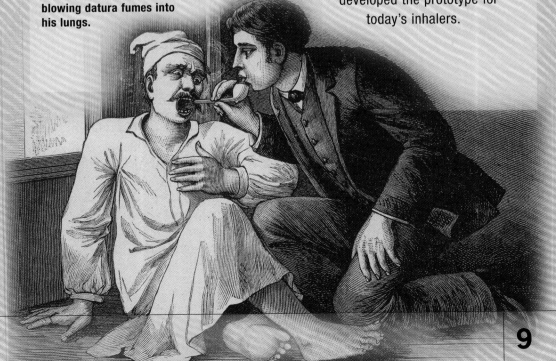

This 19th-century doctor is trying to cure his asthmatic patient by blowing datura fumes into his lungs.

Understanding asthma

When doctors first tried to treat asthma their aim was to treat the wheezing and breathlessness. But, as they began to understand more about the causes of asthma and what was happening in the lungs of people with the disease, they wanted to prevent asthma attacks, not just treat the symptoms.

Taking a closer look

First, doctors needed to take a closer look inside the airways. X-rays taken from outside the lungs told doctors little about the tiny tubes inside. In the 1960s, scientists developed miniature telescopes. These revolutionary instruments are routinely used today to look inside the lungs, the intestines and other hollow places in the body. The type used to see the airways is called a **bronchoscope**. Inside each scope is a bundle of long, thin, flexible glass fibres that carry light. The doctor inserts the bronchoscope into the patient's mouth and down into their lungs.

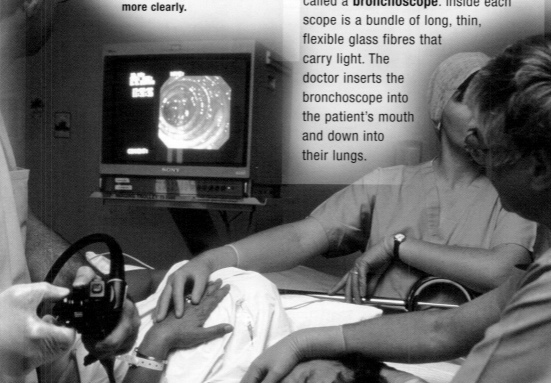

Doctors use a bronchoscope to see a patient's airways more clearly.

They can then watch what is happening through eyepieces on the end of the scope or on a large TV screen.

When doctors first started looking inside the airways of people with asthma, they were amazed at what they saw. White **mucus** plugs were blocking many of the air tubes (see pages 14–15). When these were removed surgically, the patients' breathing improved. Doctors were able to examine the mucus plugs under the microscope. They learned much more about the different cells that were getting into the airways of their asthmatic patients, making them swollen and **inflamed**.

Before long, doctors realized that it was not enough simply to treat asthma with drugs that would make the airway muscles relax. They also needed to stop mucus building up in the airways in order to prevent further attacks from occurring. For that, they needed to know much more about the role of the **immune system** (the body's natural defence against infection) in asthma and the cells that cause **inflammation** and mucus. Over 40 years later, they are still learning.

Some famous people who had asthma

Many famous historical figures have also been asthma sufferers, including:

- Ludwig van Beethoven, composer
- Che Guevara, South American revolutionary leader
- Charles Dickens, English novelist
- John F. Kennedy, 35th President of the USA (pictured below).

What is asthma?

Asthma is a condition in which the airways become temporarily obstructed, so that it is difficult to breathe air in and out. When we breathe in, air travels down the throat to the lungs through a tube called the **trachea**. Just before it reaches the lungs, the trachea splits into two tubes, called the **bronchi**, one to each lung. Inside the lungs, the bronchi branch into smaller and smaller airways, called **bronchioles**. At the end of the smallest bronchioles are tiny air sacs, called **alveoli**. These sacs are covered with tiny blood vessels. **Oxygen** from the air passes through the alveoli walls into the bloodstream. **Carbon dioxide** passes back into the lungs through the alveoli walls and is breathed out.

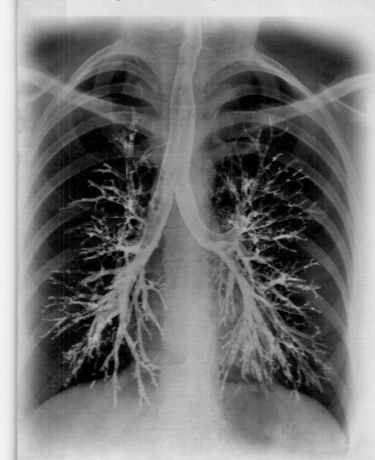

This scan of clear airways in healthy lungs shows the trachea (top), the two bronchi and the network of bronchioles.

Breathing

We breathe in and out in response to messages from the brain. Nerves carry these messages to the chest muscles between the ribs and the **diaphragm** (a sheet of muscle beneath the lungs). When it is time to breathe in, the brain tells the chest muscles to pull the ribcage outwards and the diaphragm downwards. This allows air to fill the lungs. When it is time to breathe out, the diaphragm moves upwards and air is pushed out of the lungs.

An asthma attack

An asthma attack happens when the airways tighten and close up, usually because they over-react to something in the air, such as dust, pollen, cigarette smoke or cold air. The airways become **inflamed** and swollen, and a sticky substance called **mucus** may be produced.

When the airways become narrower, less air can get in and out of the lungs. The brain registers that there is too much carbon dioxide in the blood and sends signals to the chest muscles to work harder. Breathing speeds up but it becomes very inefficient. The breaths are quick, shallow and wheezy. If you watch someone having an asthma attack you will see their chest heaving, struggling to make their chest space larger. But this does not make the airways any wider.

"The worst thing is when you have to go to the hospital. That's what happened to me when I was running around outside, playing with a friend and I didn't take my medicines. We went into his house and his cat triggered my asthma. I had a really bad attack. Now I know if I don't do what I'm supposed to, I'll have an attack and it's no fun, believe me."

(Sky Gardipe, aged 12, Kunsberg School, www.njc.org/news/healthtips/asthma_management.html)

What causes an attack?

Asthma attacks usually happen because the airways become over-sensitive when they come into contact with certain substances. For most people, pollen grains, house-dust mite droppings (see pages 20–21), cold air, animal fur and skin flakes (**dander**), and other particles pass in and out of their lungs without triggering any ill-effects. Even the poisons in cigarette smoke do not cause immediate breathing problems. But for people with asthma, all these things can irritate their airways and can set off an attack. These irritants are called **triggers**.

In asthmatic lungs, airborne particles may irritate nerve endings in the airways, leading to muscle **contraction** and narrowing of the **bronchioles**. They may also trigger a chain of events involving the **immune system**. The immune system behaves rather like an army. It controls battalions of different types of white blood cell that defend the body from attack by **bacteria**, **viruses** and other **microbes**. Some of these cells are always present in the body, while others are only produced in response to a specific attack.

Different types of asthma

The white blood cells of many people with asthma respond not only to attack by microbes, but also to harmless particles. This type of asthma is called allergic asthma. When the white blood cells appear in the airways, they activate processes that make the airways **inflamed** and swollen. Healthy airways are lined with a thin layer of sticky fluid called **mucus**. During an asthma attack, however, too much mucus is produced. This builds up in the airways, so there is even less space for air to pass through. The combination of muscle contraction, **inflammation** and tubes clogged with mucus leads to coughing and breathing problems.

There is another type of asthma, called exercise-induced asthma. Scientists are not sure what causes this type of asthma, which affects some people only after physical exertion. For people with this type of asthma, running to catch a bus, playing football or baseball, or sprinting on a track may trigger an attack. Often the situation is made worse when they are running into a wind or the air is cold. Whatever the cause, the result is the same: the airways' muscle contracts, the airways become narrower and breathing becomes difficult.

Other things, such as stressful events, can make asthma worse. When people with asthma are worried, excited, unhappy or frightened this can affect their breathing. Scientists do not really know why this happens.

Some people with asthma find that their symptoms are only triggered after exercise.

The effects of asthma

How it feels

Wheezing, coughing, shortness of breath and a tight chest are the most common symptoms of asthma, but people describe attacks in different ways. Some attacks are sudden and quite scary. This is Jenny's story.

Jenny's story

'It happens the moment I go into a smoky room. I take a few breaths and I can feel my lungs seizing up. It's as if someone has put a band around my chest and is pulling it tight. In a minute or two I start to gasp and cough. My breaths get shorter and I can hear the wheeze. Before long, it's a real effort to breathe and I just can't seem to get enough air into my lungs. I puff on my inhaler and, almost immediately, the band around my chest gets looser and I can breathe again. But I think of all that smoky air going into my lungs and decide to leave!'

Sleepless nights

Although most people with asthma describe wheezing, shortness of breath, coughing and chest tightness, the symptoms do not always happen so quickly. They can creep up, without the person realizing just how ill they are. It can be a frightening experience. Jenny describes one such attack:

'It came on slowly, so at first I hardly realized what was happening. I was staying with friends who have a cat and they always set me off. But I tried not to think about it. During dinner, I could feel my chest getting tighter. It felt like I was only breathing in the top of my lungs and nothing was getting further down.

"The best way I've heard asthma described is: 'imagine trying to breathe through a straw for five minutes. Because the straw is so narrow, it becomes very difficult to breathe air in and out.'"

(Dr Jim Wilde, paediatric emergency physician, *Augusta Chronicle*, 20 June 2002)

But it was not a big problem and my inhaler was upstairs so I just lived with it.

'Before I went to bed, I used my inhaler and my breathing improved. I was sleepy … so I dropped off quickly. Two hours later I woke with a start. It felt like there was a lump of concrete on my chest and I struggled upright to try and get some air in my lungs. I puffed on my inhaler but my chest was so tight I don't think much went down. I piled the pillows up behind me so I was sleeping sitting up. I dozed but every hour or so I woke up because I couldn't breathe. I kept puffing on my inhaler and waited till morning when I could go home.'

Inflammation

Asthma specialists used to think that, between attacks, the lungs of people with asthma looked and worked normally. But they now know that asthmatic airways are rarely entirely normal. They are nearly always red and **inflamed** – a condition called **chronic inflammation**. Sometimes the airways are so inflamed and full of **mucus** that breathing is difficult, even when there is no sign of pollen, dust or other **triggers**. At other times, the airways have only a few red or swollen patches.

In recent years, scientists have developed techniques that allow them to get remarkably detailed pictures of what happens in the airways during and between asthmatic attacks.

They can see white blood cells from the body's **immune system** arrive in the airways to 'defend' them from harmless irritants during an asthma attack. Experts have even isolated chemical messengers, such as **histamine**, that call even more misguided white blood cells into the airways.

Damage to the airway lining

Scientific research has also shown that the fragile lining of the airways becomes worn and broken up as a result of all the unnecessary immune system activity. This leaves nerve endings more exposed to passing irritants. The lungs' repair mechanisms can actually make things worse. In trying to rebuild the damaged airway lining, the walls may become thicker and stiffer than normal. This can lead to further narrowing of the airways, making breathing less efficient.

Without treatment, people who have had asthma for a long time would never breathe quite as well as those who do not have asthma. Much of the time they would hardly notice that they had a problem. But when they came in contact with an asthma trigger, ran to meet someone or walked quickly up a hill they would find it much more difficult to breathe. This is why it is so important that they take medicines not only to help them breathe more easily when they have an asthma attack, but also to prevent everyday inflammation in their lungs.

A lung scan of a person with asthma. It has been specially coloured to show normal areas (pink) and inflamed areas (yellow).

Who is affected by asthma?

Asthma is much more common in some countries than in others. The largest ever world-wide survey of asthma in children was carried out in the mid-1990s. The results showed that symptoms were 20 times more common in the UK (the country where asthma was most common) than in Indonesia (where the disease was least common). Other countries where asthma was common included New Zealand, Australia, Ireland and most of North and South America. In Eastern Europe, China, India and Ethiopia, the condition was rare.

A Western lifestyle

There are many theories why asthma is more common in developed countries than in less developed countries, but there is no definite answer. The strongest theory suggests that people in wealthier countries, such as the UK and USA, spend more time indoors and less time outside. Their homes often have fitted carpets, heavy curtains and thick fabrics on sofas and beds. Central heating keeps rooms warm and windows are rarely opened during cold weather.

A haven for house-dust mites

These living conditions are perfect, not only for humans but also for house-dust mites. These are tiny creatures that are invisible to the naked eye.

Frequent vacuuming can help reduce house-dust mites.

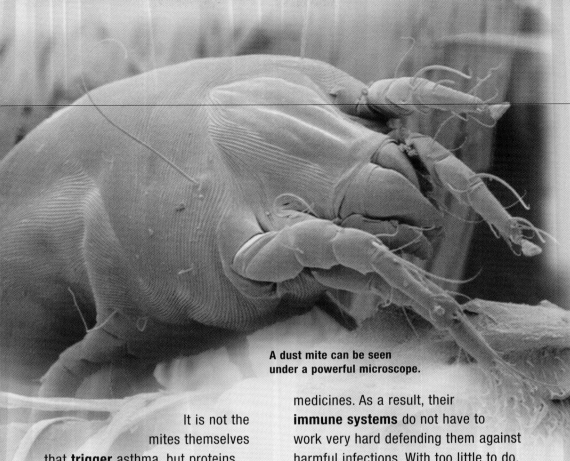

A dust mite can be seen under a powerful microscope.

It is not the mites themselves that **trigger** asthma, but proteins contained in their **faeces** (droppings). These tiny droppings can float in the air, where it is easy for people to breathe them in. In the lungs of people with asthma, this can cause irritation, leading to narrowing of the airways and **inflammation**.

There is another theory why asthma may be more common in people with higher standards of living. They are less likely to be exposed to **microbes** than those living in developing countries. In wealthier countries, children rarely get serious infections and minor infections are treated with medicines. As a result, their **immune systems** do not have to work very hard defending them against harmful infections. With too little to do, experts believe that, in some people, white blood cells (see page 14) may react to relatively harmless things in the airways, such as dust-mite faeces and pollen, attacking them and causing asthma.

In developing countries, people's immune systems do not have time to chase harmless particles in the air. They are too busy trying to fight malaria, dysentery and other life-threatening infections. And without central heating and fitted carpets, there are not many house-dust mites to do battle with.

A family connection?

People with asthma often have relatives who have the disease, too. Many people with asthma can trace the disease back through parents or grandparents, uncles or aunts, and may have cousins or more distant relatives with the condition.

Susceptibility genes?

Some illnesses, such as **cystic fibrosis** or **Huntington's disease**, are passed on from parents to children by a single faulty **gene**. Asthma is not passed on in this way – through one specific faulty gene – but it is more common in some families than in others. Scientists believe that these families carry genes called **susceptibility genes**.

They do not cause asthma by themselves but, if they are switched on (activated) by contact with **triggers** such as house-dust-mite **faeces** or pollen, they can result in asthma.

Chromosomes linked to asthma

Human genes are arranged on pairs of thread-like structures, called **chromosomes**, which lie in the centre of each cell, in the nucleus. Genes that make people susceptible to asthma have been discovered on several chromosomes.

Asthma can affect several generations of the same family.

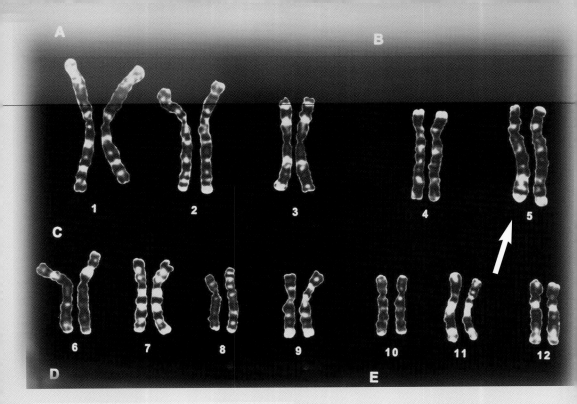

On chromosome 5 there is a cluster of genes that control the production of many of the chemical messengers that are present when the airways become **inflamed** (see pages 18–19). When these genes are switched on, they instruct cells to make proteins such as **histamine** and other messengers, which make the airways become red and swollen and lead to breathing problems.

Recently, UK and US scientists have discovered another asthma susceptibility gene, called ADAM33, on chromosome 12. Experts painstakingly examined the genes of over 400 families with a strong history of asthma. They found a link between

Scientists are researching chromosome 5 to see if it holds the key to preventing asthma.

ADAM33 and the process by which the airways of people with asthma try to repair themselves. This process can lead to thickening of the wall of the airway, further narrowing of it, and worsening of asthma symptoms.

In the next few years, researchers hope to discover other susceptibility genes for asthma. Once they understand how these genes interact with environmental factors to cause asthma, they hope one day to be able to switch them off.

Smoking and asthma

Smoking is extremely bad for asthmatic airways. Tobacco smoke contains about 300 toxic chemicals, many of which may cause cancer. Nearly all of these toxins are likely to irritate the already sensitive and fragile lining of asthmatic airways. When they do this, they make the muscles of the airways constrict so that the airways become narrower. They also **trigger** an **immune system** response that makes the airways swollen and **inflamed**.

Eight out of ten people with asthma say that smoking makes their symptoms worse. They do not even need to smoke – passive smoking (breathing in someone else's smoke) is enough to trigger an attack.

A baby whose mother smoked during pregnancy is 50 per cent more likely to have asthma or another illness caused by over-active white blood cells such as eczema, hayfever or rhinitis. When a pregnant woman inhales smoke, the poisonous chemicals enter her bloodstream through her lungs. They are then passed to the unborn child through the **placenta**. The baby's immature immune system tries to defend itself from the chemicals and, in doing so, begins a life-long battle that damages the airways and leads to asthma attacks. It is possible that

A healthy lung (left) seen next to a smoker's lung (right).

passive smoking by pregnant women may cause asthma in their unborn children, though the evidence for this is less clear.

Long-term problems

Smoking has other long-term hazards for asthmatic airways. The white blood cells gather in the airways in response to tobacco smoke. They release substances that slowly break down lung tissue, leaving it soft and soggy, like a wet sponge. This can lead to a condition called **chronic obstructive pulmonary disease (COPD)**, in which breathing can become so difficult that people may need to receive regular **oxygen** through a face-mask. All smokers are prone to COPD, but the risk is greater for those with asthma.

Kicking the habit

People who smoke are addicted to a chemical in tobacco called nicotine, which makes it difficult for them to give up. Using a nicotine replacement treatment such as nicotine chewing gum or skin patches doubles a smoker's chances of successfully giving up cigarettes. The gum and patches give the body a small, controlled dose of nicotine to relieve the craving, but avoid the other poisonous chemicals found in tobacco.

A drug called bupropion can also help people stop smoking. This is not a nicotine replacement treatment but works in the brain to reduce people's craving for nicotine.

Pollution and asthma

Could the big world-wide increase in asthma, especially in developed countries, be due to a rise in pollution levels? Scientists have been trying to answer this question for over a decade, but they are still not sure. Most are convinced that polluted air **triggers** symptoms in people who already have asthma. But it is difficult to prove whether pollution actually causes asthma because so many other factors, such as **genes**, smoking, house-dust mites and other triggers, seem to have an impact.

Research in the UK has shown that children with asthma who live close to busy roads wheeze more than those who live in less polluted areas. But children living in polluted parts of what used to be East Germany are less likely to have asthma than those living in wealthier, cleaner West Germany! Asthma is also common in countries such as New Zealand, where pollution levels are low.

"It is clearly time to get serious about enforcing all of the provisions of the Clean Air Act so that we place Americans' health above business and political interests."

A recent study carried out at the University of Southern California, USA, suggested that pollution, particularly traffic fumes, may cause asthma. The study looked at the effects of the air pollutant, **ozone**, on over 3500 children who did not have asthma. Those who played a lot of sport in areas where there was a lot of ozone were three times more likely to get asthma symptoms than children in cleaner areas with low ozone levels. Less active children were also more at risk in polluted areas, but to a lesser extent than those who did a lot of exercise and consequently breathed in more polluted air. But some scientists still do not feel there is enough proof to say that pollution causes asthma.

What you may be breathing

Over 142 million Americans are breathing unhealthy amounts of ozone, according to the American Lung Association's *State of the Air 2002* report. Six out of ten of the most ozone-polluted areas were in California, with areas of Texas, Tennessee, Georgia, and North and South Carolina also coming high in the league tables.

These people in Beijing, China, are wearing masks to protect themselves from the effects of pollution.

Treatment of asthma

There are many different medicines available to treat asthma. Relievers make it easier for people to breathe when they have asthma symptoms. Preventers are taken to reduce the likelihood of a person having the symptoms.

Relieving symptoms

All reliever drugs are designed to make the muscle around the airways relax so that air can get in and out of the lungs more easily. These drugs are called **bronchodilators**. They reduce wheezing, shortness of breath and the tight feeling in the chest

during an asthma attack. The most widely used bronchodilator is called salbutamol (albuterol in the USA). Like most other reliever drugs, people with asthma inhale salbutamol when they have symptoms. It goes straight into their airways, where it makes the muscle relax so that the airways become wider. However, reliever drugs do not reduce the **inflammation** and swelling in the airways.

Asthma inhalers come in many shapes and sizes.

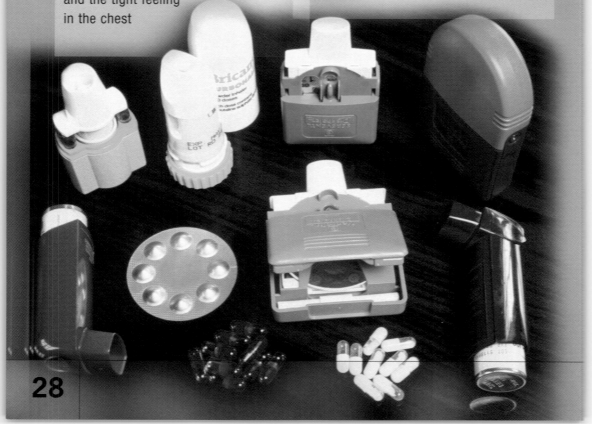

28

Short-acting relievers

Some reliever drugs are short acting while others are longer acting. When someone with asthma takes a short-acting drug, their wheezing and other symptoms improve almost immediately. The effects usually last for a few hours. People take short-acting bronchodilator drugs for immediate relief of symptoms during an asthma attack.

Long-acting relievers

A longer-acting bronchodilator will not give immediate relief. It may take 15–20 minutes before a person's airways get wider and their breathing improves. But the effects of these drugs last longer, for up to 12 hours. People tend to use longer-acting bronchodilators as additional treatment to preventer drugs (see pages 30–31). Long-acting bronchodilators can be particularly useful for people who wake up at night because of their asthma. A short-acting reliever will only help their symptoms for part of the night, while a longer-acting drug will relieve their wheezing all night, so that their sleep is not disturbed.

Keeping an eye on the condition

If the answer to any of these questions is 'yes', a person's asthma treatment may not be working as well as it should be:
- Does the person have difficulty sleeping because of asthma symptoms (including coughing)?
- Are the usual symptoms present during the day (cough, chest tightness, wheeze and breathlessness)?
- Does asthma interfere with activities?

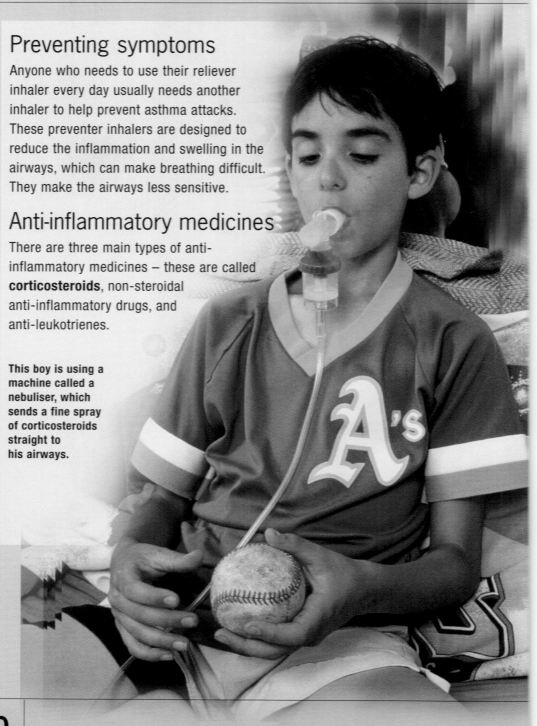

Preventing symptoms

Anyone who needs to use their reliever inhaler every day usually needs another inhaler to help prevent asthma attacks. These preventer inhalers are designed to reduce the inflammation and swelling in the airways, which can make breathing difficult. They make the airways less sensitive.

Anti-inflammatory medicines

There are three main types of anti-inflammatory medicines – these are called **corticosteroids**, non-steroidal anti-inflammatory drugs, and anti-leukotrienes.

This boy is using a machine called a nebuliser, which sends a fine spray of corticosteroids straight to his airways.

Corticosteroids interfere with the way white blood cells are activated in the airways. Non-steroidal drugs stabilize white blood cells in the airways when they come across **triggers** such as pollen or animal fur. Anti-leukotrienes are the newest group of preventer drugs used for asthma. Taken in tablet form, they block the activity of a group of chemical messengers (known as leukotrienes) that call white blood cells into the airways and trigger inflammation.

Most people with asthma find corticosteroids are the most effective way of preventing attacks. Non-steroidal drugs can prevent asthma attacks in children but are less effective in adults, and anti-leukotrienes work very well for some people with asthma, but not for others. People with asthma may need to try different types of treatment to find out which works best for them.

Side effects?

Some people prefer to avoid corticosteroids, because of the small risk of side effects. Corticosteroids are quite different from the anabolic steroids that some athletes use to improve their performance. Anabolic steroids can seriously damage the liver and other organs. But some people do still worry that corticosteroids can make bones fragile or stunt children's growth. These side effects have been seen when people with severe asthma need to take high doses of corticosteroid tablets. But such problems are extremely rare for the vast majority of people with asthma. They take only low doses of inhaled corticosteroids, and the medicine goes straight to the airways where it is needed, so very little is absorbed by the rest of the body.

Working behind the scenes

It is important that people take preventer medicines for asthma every day, even when they have no symptoms and feel very well. Unlike reliever inhalers, preventer drugs do not affect symptoms immediately. Instead, they work behind the scenes, keeping the **immune system** under control so there is less risk of asthma symptoms.

Using inhalers

Using inhalers to treat asthma ensures that medicines get straight to where they are needed – in the lungs. They work faster than tablets, which is especially important for relieving the symptoms of an asthma attack. Using an inhaler is not as easy as it looks. A doctor or asthma nurse needs to show people how to use their inhalers, and check that they are getting it right and delivering the medicine effectively. Different types of inhaler are colour-coded to make sure that people select the correct one in the event of a sudden attack.

Metered dose inhalers (MDIs)

The most widely used type of inhaler is called a metered dose inhaler, or MDI, and it is probably the most difficult type to use correctly. In MDIs, the drug is dissolved in a liquid, called a propellant, inside a small canister. It comes out of the inhaler as a fine mist, like an air freshener or deodorant spray.

To get the medicine from an MDI into the lungs, the user has to press down on the canister and breathe in at the same time. It is important to take a long, slow breath rather than a short, sharp one. Then the user has to hold their breath with their mouth closed for about 10 seconds. This helps the medicine to go down into the lungs, not get stuck in the throat or breathed out into the air.

Dry powder inhalers

Dry powder inhalers need less co-ordination. Once the mouthpiece of the inhaler is in the mouth, the drug is automatically released in the form of a powder on breathing in. But quite a deep breath is needed to activate the inhaler and get the medicine into the lungs.

Breath-actuated metered dose inhalers

There is a third type of device, called a breath-actuated metered dose inhaler. Like the MDI, the asthma medicine comes out of the inhaler as a fine mist. But, like the dry powder inhaler, the drug comes out when the user breathes in. So with this device there is no need to co-ordinate breathing with pressing the inhaler.

Spacers

For those people who find it difficult to use any of the inhaler devices, there is another option. Their medicine can be sprayed into a large, balloon-like device, called a spacer, and they can then breathe in and out normally from this until the medicine reaches their lungs.

A spacer helps people who find it difficult to use inhalers.

Taking control

No one with asthma should suffer in silence. They should not have to put up with breathing problems that get in the way of their everyday life. People with asthma should be able to go to school or work, play sport, see their friends and go on holiday just like anyone else. Most of the time, the preventer inhaler should keep asthma under control and, if a person does have an attack, their reliever inhaler should soon stop them wheezing.

But taking control of asthma can take a little time and effort. As with any health problem, people need to get to know their asthma. They need to know what makes it worse or better, how to monitor their breathing, and when to adapt their treatment to how they are feeling.

People who control their asthma can take part in most sporting activities.

Monitoring symptoms

There are various ways to check how the lungs are performing. Breathing problems are clearly a good guide to whether treatment is working. Anyone who needs to use their reliever inhaler more than once a day because they are wheezing or short of breath should tell their doctor or asthma nurse. They may need to change the dose of their preventer inhaler medicine or the type of drug they are taking.

People can also measure how well their lungs are working. At home, they can use a device called a peak-flow meter, usually when they wake up and before they go to bed. They take a deep breath and blow into the meter as hard as they can. The breath pushes a small indicator up the side of the device. This shows a person's peak expiratory flow (the full force of their outward breath). If the reading is consistently lower than recommended by their doctor, they may need to change their treatment.

The doctor can measure how well a person's lungs are working more accurately using a device called

A peak-flow meter shows how hard a person can breathe air out of their lungs.

a **spirometer** (see pages 8–9). Again, this involves blowing into the device as hard as possible and this gives a reading of the maximum amount of air a person can breathe out in one second.

No one should change their asthma treatment without talking to their doctor first. Many people with asthma work out treatment plans with their doctor or asthma nurse. These plans show them how to reduce their medicine if their asthma is better, or increase it if their symptoms are getting worse.

Living with asthma

Asthma can affect all areas of a person's everyday life – if they let it. It can keep some people away from school, make them avoid doing sport or even playing with friends. It can make them think twice about going to parties and social events. It can even stop them sleeping, so they feel washed-out and tired in the morning.

Giving in to asthma?

Surveys consistently show that people with asthma allow their disease to have too much impact on their life. They get so used to its limitations that they do not expect to feel as well as they should. When their wheezing keeps them awake at night, they do not go to their doctor or asthma nurse and tell them about it. When they get wheezy and out of breath playing football with their mates, they drop out and make excuses the next time they are asked to play, instead of getting better treatment so they can take part.

Asthma specialists are urging people with this condition not to be embarrassed about getting help and, just as important, to stop accepting second-best.

Even so, some people with asthma are still unwilling to admit or accept that they are having difficulties. They do not feel comfortable with going back to their doctor when things are not going well.

Young people may feel it is not cool to carry an inhaler around with them and they may not want to draw attention to themselves by using it in public. Puffing on an inhaler is not a sign of weakness or being abnormal. It just means that a person does not want their breathing problems to affect their life and are taking control of their asthma.

"I told my new friends about my asthma and they were always very understanding. It just meant that they had to get used to sitting in non-smoking sections of pubs and clubs, but I don't think they minded too much."

(Sallie Robinson, UK National Asthma Campaign/Real Lives)

37

Avoiding triggers

People with asthma should avoid things that **trigger** their attacks. Some people know what makes them wheeze. If they go into a dusty room, or pick up a friend's cat, they can feel their chest getting tighter.

House-dust mites

House-dust mites are probably the most common trigger for asthma symptoms. Invisible to the naked eye, they are everywhere in the home, especially in carpets, curtains, bedding and soft toys. The best way to avoid them is to have wood floors instead of carpets, and blinds instead of curtains. All bedding should be washed at 60 ºC, rooms should be vacuumed frequently and kept well ventilated. Protective covers on mattresses may reduce the likelihood that a person will be sleeping with dust mites!

Pollen

Tree and grass pollen can trigger asthma. Some people are only affected by certain types of pollen, while others wheeze as soon as they go into a garden or field. When driving through the countryside during the pollen season, they should keep car windows shut. If flowers make someone with asthma wheeze, they should keep them out of the home, especially bedrooms.

Pets

Doctors used to tell people with asthma to get rid of pets if they made them wheeze. But it is not easy to give away the family cat or dog! However, keeping pets out of bedrooms may help. Sleeping with a dog on the bed or a hamster in the room is the worst thing a person with asthma can do. If they touch an animal or bird, they should always wash their hands afterwards, before touching their face or mouth. That can reduce the chance of animal hair, skin or feather particles (**dander**) getting into their lungs and making them wheeze.

Interestingly, recent research has suggested that having a cat from an early age can actually protect children from developing asthma when there is a family history of **allergy**. It seems that their **immune systems** get used to cat dander. This means that if particles get into their lungs, they do not wheeze.

Wooden floors do not trap as much dust as carpets and can help prevent asthma symptoms.

Jackie Joyner-Kersee's story

Six-time Olympic gold medallist Jackie Joyner-Kersee risked her life by failing to accept that she had asthma. It was not until a near-fatal attack in 1993 that she started to take the condition seriously.

Diagnosed at eighteen, when she was at college, American athlete Jackie did not want her asthma to interfere with her growing reputation as a top athlete. She thought that if people knew she had the condition she would not be allowed to fulfil her true potential.

'I refused to accept it and hid it from my coaches and team-mates. But ignoring the problem didn't make it go away,' she recalled in an article in the newspaper, *USA Today*.

Failing to take her medication regularly landed Jackie in hospital several times during her record-breaking years as a top sprinter. She would take her drugs when she was not feeling well, but as soon as she felt better again she dropped the medication. In the end, it was the very serious attack in 1993 that finally convinced her to get effective treatment – and to continue taking it even when she felt really good.

'It was like a pillow had been shoved over my face. I'll never forget the panic of being completely unable to breathe, no matter how hard I tried,' she said.

Fortunately, doctors were able to save Jackie and give her emergency medication to help her breathe again. In 1998, she retired from competition and, since then, she has been spreading the word about how important it is for people to keep their asthma under control.

'My denial and irresponsible attitude about asthma put me at great risk and caused me so much needless suffering. My hope is that the kids I talk to learn to open up about their asthma, become educated about their condition, and seek help,' she says. 'There are few restrictions on your life with asthma, as long as you take care of yourself.'

When the worst happens

Unfortunately, a few people have severe asthma attacks, even if they take their medicine regularly. In the very worst cases, such attacks can be life-threatening.

Charlotte Coleman was the waif-like actress who played the part of Hugh Grant's flat-mate, Scarlet, in a popular film, *Four Weddings and a Funeral*. Charlotte's career went from strength to strength during the 1990s but, on 17 November 2001, she died following a severe asthma attack at the age of 33. It appeared that either she was unable to use her reliever inhaler or did not respond to it. Her family reported that she had been feeling unwell the day before she died.

Just two months earlier, a severe asthma attack took the life of world-renowned South African Surgeon, Dr Christiaan Barnard. Barnard had performed the first successful heart transplant operation in 1967. Holidaying in Cyprus, Barnard appears to have had an asthma attack the day before his death, and was grappling with his inhaler before losing consciousness on the day he died.

British actress, Charlotte Coleman.

Warning signs

Each year, over 4500 people in the USA and about 1500 in the UK die as a result of their asthma. There are thousands more deaths around the world. Although asthma deaths, like those of Charlotte Coleman and Christiaan Barnard, are usually sudden and shocking, there are often warning signs in the days and weeks beforehand. Research has shown that in fatal cases of asthma, people have had many more asthma attacks and needed to use their reliever inhalers much more than usual in the days or weeks leading up to their death. When asthma is very severe, the airways become so narrow that it becomes very difficult for the person to inhale their reliever medication well enough to get it into their lungs.

Emergency treatment

Worsening asthma symptoms or serious attacks should never be ignored. Anyone who is not responding to their reliever inhaler should get emergency treatment in hospital, especially if their asthma has been getting worse in the previous days or weeks. In hospital, they can have injections of asthma drugs that get to their lungs through their bloodstream and therefore bypass their blocked airways. They can also breathe in their asthma drugs through a face-mask attached to a machine, so that they do not need to breathe deeply for the medication to reach their lungs.

ll a cure be found?

ture, if doctors could
e asthma earlier – perhaps
fore children are born – they
e able to stop them ever
g or being short of breath.

diagnosis?

already test babies in the
r soon after they are born for
of **genetic** disorders, such as
ibrosis, if they suspect the
might be at risk. Doctors
cure these diseases but, by
ing them early, they can often
the amount of damage they
e body and relieve symptoms
as they start to appear.

enetic tests are developed for
, they may enable children to
eatment to damp down their
ve **immune system** from an
e. This would stop their
becoming swollen and
d. The cycle of irritation,
nation, airway narrowing and
g would then be broken.

Taking extra care

Scientists have already discovered
that, even in the womb, a baby with
asthma **genes** can be susceptible to
what its mother breathes and eats.
If there is a family history of **allergies**
and the baby is exposed to **triggers**
through the mother's blood supply in
the womb, the baby is likely to show
signs of allergies and asthma at an
early age. This is especially true
during the second half of pregnancy.
If parents knew that their unborn child
had genes for asthma, they could be
especially careful about exposing him
or her to dust, pollen, cigarette smoke
or other particles that might trigger
an attack.

No woman is likely to be able to
avoid all asthma triggers while she is
pregnant. But, if she can reduce her
baby's exposure to the worst triggers
during pregnancy, her child's asthma
genes may not be switched on (see
pages 22–23).

By understanding ... asthma, how it begins, and how genes and environment interact, real progress is being made ... in the next ten years, I expect to see huge changes in how people with asthma cope with everyday life.

(Professor Stephen Holgate, *Science Today, Health Tomorrow* lectures at the Royal Institution, London, 2001)

45

New treatments

Most of the research into new treatments for asthma is looking for better ways to prevent inflammation in the airways rather than to relieve the symptoms of asthma attacks. The drugs that are today used to reduce inflammation in the airways affect many different types of white blood cells, including those that are not important in asthma. Doctors would like new treatments that target only the cells that cause the most trouble in asthma. To do this, they need to find out more about the chief culprits.

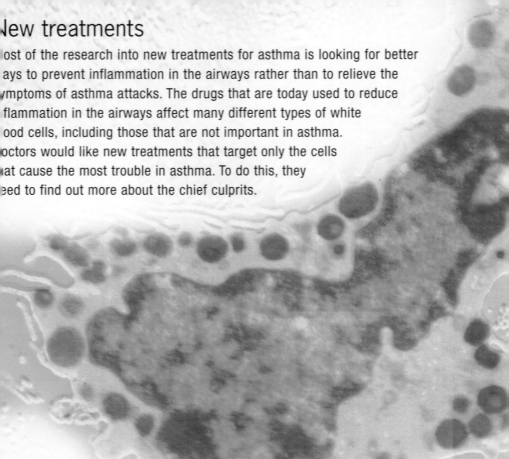

A cell releases histamines, which cause inflammation, in response to an asthma trigger.

Like detectives investigating a group of criminals, scientists need to know which are the ringleaders amongst the white blood cells that cause asthma, who are their informers and middlemen, and who does their dirty work. They know most of the key players in airway inflammation and some of the messengers that the white cells use to bring in reinforcements. But scientists now need to develop drugs that will deal with the ones that play the biggest role in the way inflammation builds up in the airways. It will take a lot of work. Identifying the main culprits is only the first step. Finding new drugs that can deal with them is likely to be very difficult. Any new drug has to be carefully tested – first on volunteers and then on people with asthma – to make sure it is safe and it works. For each new treatment that comes on to the market, thousands are discarded along the way.

The first new treatment due to come on to the market is a drug called omalizumab (also known as Xolair). This drug targets one of the 'asthma middlemen'. Omalizumab binds to and effectively 'arrests' an **antibody** called IgE. By stopping IgE from over-reacting to pollen, dust and other particles, and alarming other white cells, omalizumab may damp down inflammation before it becomes serious. At first it will only be used in people with the most serious asthma. But, as doctors learn more about it, this type of treatment may be adapted for milder asthma.

IgE is not the only middleman in the immune system. Many other agents over-react to harmless particles in the air and trigger asthma attacks. Doctors need to be able to neutralize these as well – without damaging the body's normal defences against infection.

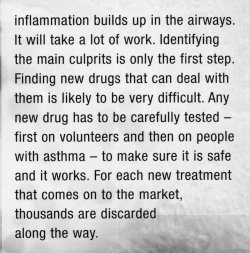

Pollen from some flowers and grasses can trigger an over-reaction from white blood cells, leading to inflammation of the airways of a person with asthma.

New challenges

One of the biggest challenges for today's asthma scientists involves reprogramming the body's immune system so that it no longer over-reacts to harmless particles in the air. Their main target is a large family of white blood cells called T lymphocytes. There are two main types of T lymphocytes – killer T cells and helper T cells.

As the name suggests, killer T cells are the immune system's hitmen. They kill invading **microbes**, but they need instructions from helper T cells in order to do this. Scientists know that there are at least three types of helper T cells – Th1, Th2 and Th0. Th1 cells target fairly lightweight microbes, such as **viruses**, Th2 cells recognize more heavyweight microbes, such as worms, and Th0 cells may turn into either Th1 or Th2 cells.

In developed countries, where hygiene standards are high, Th2 cells rarely need to seek out worm infections. With so little work to do, Th2 cells appear to have gradually adapted to recognize and attack pollen, dust and other harmless particles. Experts believe that people with asthma may have an imbalance of T cells, producing too few Th1 and too many Th2 cells. Scientists are trying to find ways of re-programming their immune systems so that they produce more Th1 cells and fewer Th2.

Killer T cells like this one destroy invading microbes and substances identified by helper T cells.

Learning from nature

For this, they are learning from nature. Asthma seems to be less common in children who are still exposed to above average risk of infection. For example, families who farm in a rather old-fashioned way in parts of Germany, living in the same building as their animals, do not have much asthma. Certain families in Sweden who live a simple life and do not use many modern medicines also have low levels of asthma. It seems that, by giving these children's immune systems plenty to do, combating the infections they were designed to prevent, these families have inadvertently protected them from asthma.

What scientists now need to do is to find a way, with drugs or vaccines, to mimic this protective effect. They would like to re-programme the immune systems of children who are at risk of getting asthma. But they will have to be very careful that, by changing one group of white blood cells, they do not upset the delicate balance of some other part of the defence system.

Amish people in the US farm without the help of machinery. This simple lifestyle where people work closely with their animals may help reduce the likelihood of developing asthma.

Will a cure be found?

Gene therapy?

such as cystic fibrosis. But finding the

Curing asthma with gene therapy is unlikely to be an option for anyone who has the disease today. And there are potentially grave risks. One child who had gene therapy to correct an immune deficiency disease now has leukaemia. This could mean that, by correcting the abnormal gene that was preventing the child's white blood cells from combating infection, the treatment has damaged another part of their immune system, causing leukaemia.

Looking to the future

Today we have drugs that effectively treat asthma symptoms and drugs that can help reduce their frequency. We also know many of the things that trigger asthma and how to avoid them. For most people with asthma, the days when the disease severely restricted their everyday lives should now be over. But finding a cure is likely to test the ingenuity of researchers for several decades.

A gene therapy success story

A small number of children are born with a genetic defect that means they have no immune system to defend them from colds, flu and other common infections. Until recently, they died within a few years as a result of an infection that might keep the rest of us in bed for only a day or two. After gene therapy to correct the faulty gene they have started to produce the white blood cells they need to protect them from disease.

Scientists are looking for a way to use gene therapy to cure asthma.

Information and advice

Many organizations offer information about living with asthma and have helplines people can call for further information.

Contacts in the UK

National Asthma Campaign
Tel: 020 7226 2260
The Asthma Helpline: 0845 7 01 02 03
(Mondays to Fridays 9 a.m.–5 p.m.)
Providence House, Providence Place
London N1 0NT
Website: www.asthma.org.uk
Dedicated to conquering asthma by funding research to improve treatments and find a cure for the future. It offers independent help and advice to everyone affected by asthma and campaigns for a better deal for people with asthma. The confidential helpline is staffed by asthma nurses, who provide up-to-date advice, and can discuss any concerns.

British Lung Foundation
78 Hatton Garden, London EC1N 8LD
Tel: 020 7831 5831
Website: www.lunguk.org
This is a charity in the UK that funds research into the prevention, diagnosis, treatment and cure of all lung diseases, including asthma, and provides information and support to people with these conditions, and to their families.

Contacts in the USA

American Lung Association
61 Broadway, 6th floor, New York, NY 10006
Tel: 212 315 8700
Website: www.lungusa.org
An organization with the mission of preventing lung disease and promoting lung health, it has extensive information on lung diseases, including asthma.

Asthma & Allergy Foundation of America
1233 Twentieth Street, NW, Suite 402
Washington DC 20036, USA
Tel: 800 727-8462 or +1 (202) 466-7643
Website: www.aafa.org
This is a non-profit organization dedicated to finding a cure for and controlling asthma and allergy related diseases through the support of research, patient and public education programmes, and a network of support groups.

Just for kids
Website: www.aaaai.org/patients/just4kids/
This is a special website for parents and children with asthma, developed by the American Academy of Allergy, Asthma and Immunology, a group mainly for doctors and scientists with an interest in asthma and other allergic conditions.

Allergy and Asthma Network Mothers of Asthmatics AANMA
Website: www.aanma.org/
This website provides extensive information about asthma for families and anyone who wants to know more about the illness.

Contacts in Australia and New Zealand

Asthma Australia
National Office
Level 3, 63 Stead Street
South Melbourne VIC 3205.
Tel: 03 9696 7861
Fax: 03 9696 7397
Email: national@asthma.org.au.
Website: www.asthmaaustralia.org.au

Asthma Foundations
Tel: 1800 645 130
An association of all the Asthma Foundations throughout Australia, with the aim of eliminating asthma as a major cause of ill health and disruption within the community.

National Asthma Campaign
Level 1, 1 Palmerston Crescent,
South Melbourne, Victoria 3205
Tel: 03 9214 1476
Fax: 03 9214 1400
Website: www.NationalAsthma.org.au
A non-profit organization that creates awareness and provides information about asthma.

The Asthma and Respiratory Foundation of New Zealand (Inc.)
P O Box 1459, Wellington
Tel: +64 4 499 4592
Fax: +64 4 499 4594
Email: arf@asthmanz.co.nz
A national non-governmental organization which aims to help people with asthma and respiratory conditions.

Further Reading

The Asthma Handbook, by Jenny Lewis; Vermilion (an imprint of Ebury Press), 1995

Health Issues: Asthma, by Sarah Lennard-Brown; Hodder Wayland, 2002

Living with Asthma, by Peta Bee; Hodder Wayland, 1998

Asthma and Allergies for Dummies, by Dr W. Berger; IDG Worldwide Inc, 2000

Breathe Easy, by J. H. Weiss; Magination Press, 1994

I'm Tougher than Asthma, by S. M. Carter and A.R. Carter; Albert Whitman and Co, 1996

Taking Charge of Asthma, by Dr B. B. Wray; John Wiley and Sons Inc, 1998

Disclaimer
All the Internet addresses (URLs) given in this book were valid at the time of going to press. However, due to the dynamic nature of the Internet, some addresses may have changed, or sites may have changed or ceased to exist since publication. While the author and Publisher regret any inconvenience this may cause readers, no responsibility for any such changes can be accepted by either the author or the Publisher.

Glossary

adrenaline
a substance that increases heart rate and blood pressure and also affects the airways

allergy
an abnormal over-reaction of the immune system to something in the air (such as pollen), certain types of food or other triggers (such as bee stings)

alveoli
air sacs in the lungs. They are covered with thin-walled blood vessels that allow gases to get in and out of the bloodstream.

antibody
a blood protein released by the body in response to an asthma trigger such as pollen or animal dander

bacteria
microbes that can cause infections (for example some types of food poisoning, and chest and urinary infections)

bronchi (singular bronchus)
the two main tubes into the lungs

bronchioles
small tubes in the lungs which branch off the bronchi

bronchodilators
medicines that relax the airways and make them wider

bronchoscope
a medical instrument used for looking at a person's airways

carbon dioxide
a gas that makes up about 0.04 per cent of air. Carbon dioxide, together with water, is a waste product of a chemical process in the body called respiration, which releases energy from within cells.

chromosomes
structures in cells that carry a person's genes

chronic
long lasting

chronic obstructive pulmonary disease (COPD)
a serious lung disease, also called bronchitis or emphysema

contract
become smaller and tighter (for example muscles contract when they are active)

corticosteroids
anti-inflammatory medicines that help prevent the airways from becoming too inflamed

cystic fibrosis
an inherited condition that affects the lungs, pancreas and other parts of the body where mucus is produced

dander
hair, skin cell and feather particles from animals and birds that can trigger an asthma attack

diaphragm
the sheet of muscle that separates the chest from the abdomen. The diaphragm is essential for breathing.

enema
a cleansing solution put into the bowel through the anus. An enema is given to wash out faeces and other debris.

ephedrine
a medicine that was used to treat asthma before more effective and safer medicines could be made

faeces
waste products from digested food (droppings)

gene
a unit of genetic material. Thousands of genes are carried on the chromosomes in human cells and provide information for the body to make proteins needed for many different jobs in the body.

gene therapy
a way of changing one or more genes in cells, usually as a treatment for a disease

genetic
inherited from a parent through the genes

histamine
a natural substance produced by the body that causes inflammation and swelling

Huntington's disease
an inherited nerve disease

immune system
the body's defence system against infection

inflamed
red, swollen, often painful

inflammation
redness and swelling

microbes
tiny organisms (living things), for example bacteria, that may cause an infection

Middle Ages
the period of European history starting in the 5th century and ending around the 14th century

mucus
a slimy fluid also called phlegm. In large amounts it can cause blockages.

oxygen
a gas that makes up 21 per cent of air. It is required by living things for the release of energy from their food.

ozone
a super-charged form of oxygen, produced when sunlight reacts with chemicals, such as those emitted in vehicle exhaust gases

pharmaceutical company
a medicine manufacturer

placenta
an organ formed in the womb during pregnancy. Oxygen and nutrients pass from the mother's bloodstream into that of the foetus and waste products pass from the foetus back into the mother's bloodstream.

Renaissance
a period of history from the 14th to the 16th centuries that saw the birth of many new ideas in science and art

spasm
overactive muscle contraction

spirometer
a device used to measure how well the lungs are working

stethoscope
a device used to listen to sounds in the chest

susceptibility gene
a gene that increases the risk of getting a disease but may not cause it directly

trachea
the large tube that carries air from the throat towards the lungs

trigger
a substance such as pollen, dust-mite faeces, or pollution, that sets off an asthma attack

viruses
tiny microbes that can cause infection (for example colds and flu)

Index

Titles in the *Need to Know* series include:

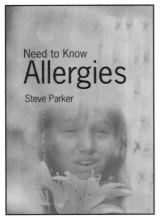

Need to Know
Allergies
Steve Parker

Hardback   0 431 09760 7

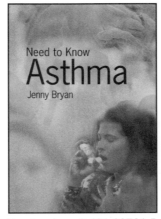

Need to Know
Asthma
Jenny Bryan

Hardback   0 431 09761 5

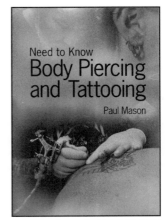

Need to Know
Body Piercing and Tattooing
Paul Mason

Hardback   0 431 09818 2

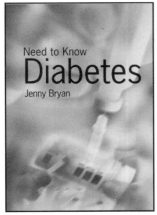

Need to Know
Diabetes
Jenny Bryan

Hardback   0 431 09762 3

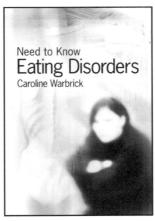

Need to Know
Eating Disorders
Caroline Warbrick

Hardback   0 431 09799 2

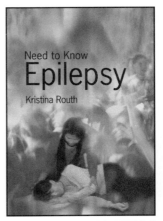

Need to Know
Epilepsy
Kristina Routh

Hardback   0 431 09763 1

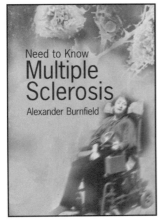

Need to Know
Multiple Sclerosis
Alexander Burnfield

Hardback   0 431 09764 X

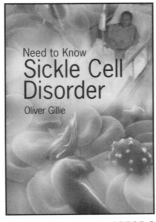

Need to Know
Sickle Cell Disorder
Oliver Gillie

Hardback   0 431 09765 8

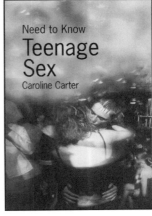

Need to Know
Teenage Sex
Caroline Carter

Hardback   0 431 09821 2

Find out about the other titles in this series on our website www.heinemann.co.uk/library